# The Extraordinary
# BOOK
## that makes you an
# ARTIST

Illustrated by
**Go Suga**

Written by
**Mary Richards**

CUT OUT and MAKE the ART PROJECTS. STORE them in the PORTFOLIO POCKET at the back of this BOOK.

**weldonowen**

# A message from Mary Richards

## Hello, extraordinary artists!

In this book, you'll find lots of art projects to assemble and do. There's something to cut out and assemble on every page—from a floating sculpture to a Bauhaus theater, from a color wheel to a cubist portrait.

On each page of the book, you'll find step-by-step instructions along with things to draw, color, cut or press out, and put together. As you read, design, and create, you'll also discover more about art techniques, movements, styles, and artists—from the surrealist artists of the 1920s to artists working today using textiles, sculpture, and collage.

## LOOK IT UP!

In every project, "Look it Up!" bubbles point to particular works of art you might like to explore further.

By the time you've finished, the book won't be a book at all—it will have turned into a handy portfolio so that you can store all your creations safely. Just turn to the back of the book to find your portfolio pocket.

So what are you waiting for? Turn the page, and enjoy!

Mary Richards spent many years working at London's Tate and Hayward galleries, making books with artists from all over the world. Now, Mary enjoys researching and writing books about art and artists, including this one!

Go Suga's artwork is a mix of abstract and graphical forms, folksy patterns and textures, and bright colors. He believes in learning by doing and develops his style all the time by painting, drawing, and trying out new techniques and materials.

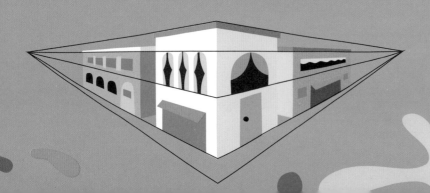

# CONTENTS

# TAKE A DOT
## for a walk

**1**

Make a drawing that "travels" between some dots.

Artist Paul Klee once described a line as "a dot that went for a walk." Put your finger on the black dot and follow the line on its journey!

Between the dots, the line loops forward and backward, and changes direction.

Adding color brings the line drawing to life.

## Keep your pencil on the paper!

**1** Grab a pencil and paper. Without thinking too much, sketch overlapping lines, loops, and spirals.

**2** Look at the design you've created. Can you make sense of your picture? (It doesn't have to make sense!)

**3** Color in parts with pencils or paints. You can color in the lines or draw shapes over the top.

### LOOK IT UP!

Paul Klee,
*Drawing Knotted in the Manner of a Net*, 1920

Hilma af Klint,
*The Seven-Pointed Star,
No. 5 and No. 7*, 1908

Use a felt-tip pen to add lines between the dots without taking your pen off the page.

# TURN THE OUTDOORS
## into art

Artists don't just stay in the studio. They like to get outside in the open air, making art with leaves, rocks, and stones.

Outdoor art is made from material found in gardens, parks, or other outdoor places.

Leaves, sticks, seed pods, or stones are great resources.

Artists make the most of different colors, shapes, and textures.

## Make outdoor art

1 Gather objects of one shape or color.

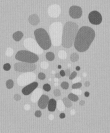

2 Combine them to make a picture.

3 Take any leftover items home to create an artwork later on.

4 You can also sketch your creation!

### LOOK IT UP!

Cecilia Vicuña, *Casa Espiral*, 1966

Andy Goldsworthy, *Pebbles Around a Hole*, 1987

# Use these cards to make some outdoor art.

Find some stones and arrange them in a line, from smallest to largest.

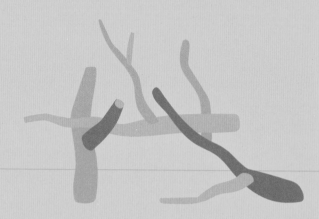

Gather some sticks. Can you make a structure that stands up on its own?

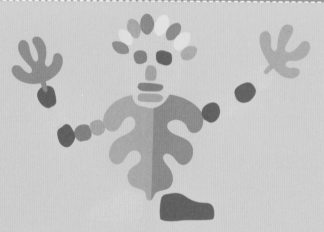

Make a nature character with some materials you find.

Gather leaves and arrange them in a spiral, starting with a pale color, and getting gradually darker.

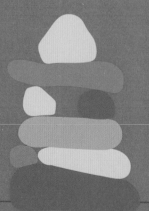

Make a tower of natural materials. Work out what balances best!

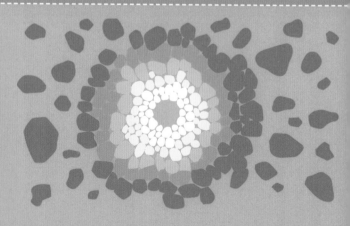

Draw a circle in the ground with a stick. Leaving the circle free, make an artwork around it.

# DRAW WITH SCISSORS
## and create a bright paper collage

A collage is a picture that combines different images. You can mix shapes that are recognizable—people, stars, waves—with others that are abstract and don't look like anything.

Use the leftovers, too—you might find some interesting shapes!

## Create a collage with paper shapes

1 Turn over and cut up the colored shapes. Or find your own paper to design and cut out your own.

2 Combine all your different shapes on a colored background and glue them on.

3 Stand back and admire!

### LOOK IT UP!

Henri Matisse, *The Parakeet and the Mermaid*, 1952

Romare Bearden, *A Black Odyssey*, 1977

Cut out these shapes and make your own Matisse-inspired collage.

Henri Matisse created collages using a technique he called "drawing with scissors." He pinned his shapes to the wall so he could see his cutouts clearly.

# DESIGN A COSTUME
## and wear it like an artist!

At the Bauhaus art school in Germany, artists lived and worked together. They loved dressing up and designing costumes for ballet and theater shows.

Favorite Bauhaus colors were black, white, blue, red, and yellow.

Bauhaus costumes were based on artists' favorite shapes—the square, the circle, and the triangle.

## Make a Bauhaus-inspired costume

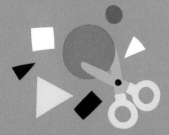

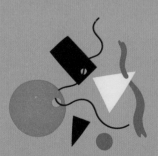

1 Find clothes in Bauhaus colors (black, white, red, blue, and yellow).

2 Cut cardboard geometric shapes—discs, squares, and triangles—and paint them.

3 Attach your Bauhaus shapes to the clothes with string, ribbon, or wool.

4 Move and dance! If you make more than one costume, put on a show with a friend.

# Use these characters to create your own Bauhaus theater.

Fold along the blue dotted lines.

These costumes were made for a Bauhaus ballet in 1922. The artist, Oskar Schlemmer, based them on geometric shapes—cylinders, cones, spheres, and spirals.

## LOOK IT UP!

Oskar Schlemmer's Costumes for the *Triadic Ballet*, 1922

Anni Albers, *Black-White-Yellow*, 1926

# USE A VIEWFINDER
## to make a composition

5
Turn over to make a viewfinder of your own.

A viewfinder helps artists to choose a scene they would like to draw. It is a great way of looking closely.

X marks the center point of the picture.

To find a good composition, move the viewfinder around!

## Make a viewfinder frame

1 Press out the frame on the next page. Find a ball of wool and some scissors.

2 Lay a length of wool over the frame diagonally, overlapping each corner.

3 Thread the wool through the hole in the top corner, and knot in place.

4 Do the same through the hole at the bottom corner.

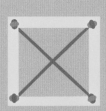

5 Lay another piece of wool diagonally over the other two corners. Thread and tie in place.

Press out the holes.

Press out your
viewfinder frame.

## Use your viewfinder frame

1 Look at different
spaces and choose
the view you'd
like to draw.

2 Use the center
point to remember
which view you've
chosen.

3 Carefully draw what you
can see. Viewfinders
are great for focusing
on small details!

### LOOK IT UP!

David Hockney,
*Woldgate Woods,* 2006

Vincent Van Gogh,
*Van Gogh's Chair,* 1888

# USE SIMPLE SHAPES
## to make a vibrant picture

Some artists make pictures from geometric shapes. They use circles to explore movement and the effects of color.

Circles can overlap or appear to move.

Cut-up circles can be arranged in different ways.

## Circles, circles, circles!

**1** Cut out the circles on the next page. You can also find circles in old magazines or draw and cut out your own!

**2** Arrange the shapes on a sheet of paper with some overlapping and some in halves.

**3** Arrange and glue your shapes onto a piece of paper.

**4** Draw around some of the shapes and add straight lines.

Cut out these circles and semicircles to make your own geometric art.

LOOK IT UP!

Sophie Taeuber-Arp,
*Rising, Flying, Falling*, 1934

Wassily Kandinsky,
*Several Circles*, 1926

# PICTURE YOURSELF
## and frame it!

A self-portrait is a picture an artist makes of themself. Self-portraits can be lifelike or include exaggerated features, bold colors, and geometric shapes.

The artist might use a mirror to look closely at their features.

## Put yourself in the picture!

1 Find a mirror and look carefully at your face.

2 Start drawing— look closely at what you see.

3 Plan a background.

4 Grab some paints— make your picture colorful.

5 Next time, you could try painting yourself in a costume or a disguise!

Press out these frames
and hang your picture
on the wall.

## LOOK IT UP!

Frida Kahlo, *Self-Portrait
with Monkey*, 1940

Peter Blake, *Self-Portrait
with Badges*, 1961

Jacob Lawrence,
*Self-Portrait*, 1977

# EXPLORE CUBISM
## and see things differently

**8**
Turn over to make your own version of this portrait.

We don't just look at things from one angle. One hundred years ago, cubist artists made pictures that took in many views at once.

A cubist portrait might include a nose viewed from the front and from the side.

The face looks very strange—all jumbled up.

Turn over. Do you recognize this face?

## Make a cubist portrait

1 Turn over to find four pictures of a face from different angles.

2 Cut out the different features so that you can rearrange them.

3 Mix up the pieces to make a cubist face.

### LOOK IT UP!

Pablo Picasso, *Bust of a Woman (Dora Maar)*, 1938

Juan Gris, *Still Life with a Guitar*, 1913

## Create a cubist picture of your own face

1 Take photos of your face from lots of different angles.

2 Include photos from close up and far away.

3 Cut up the pictures with scissors and mix them up.

4 Make a new picture. Does it still look like you?

5 You can make a cubist picture from other scenes and objects, to

# LIGHT AND SHADE
## master tone and texture

9

Try different styles of shading.

Use light and shade to get the most out of your pencil or pen. You can make a flat drawing look 3D!

You can create shadows by blending tones or by using a mix of lines.

The light source affects the ways the shadows fall on the object.

## Create shade and light

1 Find pencils, a light, and an object you'd like to draw.

2 Direct the light on one part of the object.

3 Carefully observe the shadows—where is it light and where is it dark?

4 Sketch your creation!

# Keep these guides to practice your pencil or pen skills. There are different styles of shading that you can try.

Hatching—use tiny little lines drawn close together.

Crosshatching—hatch the area, then draw lines in the opposite direction over them.

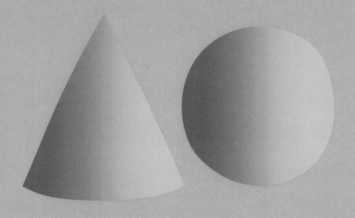

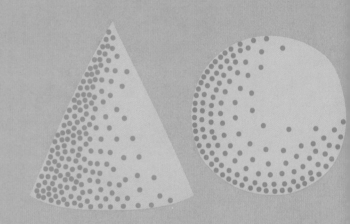

Blending—sketch smooth shades with a pencil, then blend them with your finger.

Stippling—use lots of tiny dots to make up the shaded areas.

## Practice light and dark shading

Sketching pencils are marked with numbers and letters—from H ("hard") to B ("black").

4H  3H  2H  F  HB  2B  3B  4B  5B  6B  7B  8B

### LOOK IT UP!

Vija Celmins,
*Untitled (Ocean),*
1977

Ed Ruscha,
*Pool,* 1968

# MAKE OP ART
## to boggle your brain

An optical illusion is when our eyes are fooled into thinking something is moving when it isn't. Op art pictures combine shape and color to dazzle our eyes.

The curved lines make these flat walls take on strange and unusual shapes.

Installations are works of art you can walk around in. Here, the whole room is an illusion.

## Draw a 3D hand

1 Put your hand on a piece of blank paper. Draw around it very lightly with a pencil.

2 Mark every half inch up both sides of the sheet.

3 Take a ruler and draw lines across the page, but don't draw on the hand.

4 Starting from the bottom, connect the first two lines, making a hill shape.

5 Moving up the page, connect all the lines with hill shapes, including each finger.

## Make an op art gallery

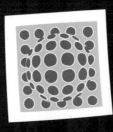

Can you see black dots appearing in

Our eyes are drawn to the shape in

Here, flower petals appear to spin round

These curved hoops make the ball

**LOOK IT UP!**

Bridget Riley,
Movement in Squares,
1961

Victor Vasarely,
Banya, 1964

# TESSELLATE
## with interlocking shapes

A tessellation is a pattern made out of shapes that fit together without leaving any space.

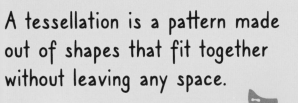

Hunt for different interlocking shapes in this picture.

Art tessellations can be made with many different shapes—squares, triangles, or even lizards!

## Create a tessellating pattern

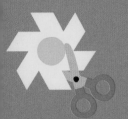

1 Cut out one of the templates on the next page.

2 Draw around the template on a clean sheet of paper.

3 Lift off the template and place it next to your outline, matching up the edges carefully.

4 Do the same again, and repeat!

5 Color your picture in bright, contrasting colors.

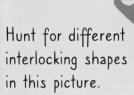

# Use these templates to make tessellating works of art.

## LOOK IT UP!

M.C. Escher, *Bird Fish*, 1938

M.C. Escher, *Reptiles*, 1943

M.C. Escher, *Regular Division of the Plane III*, 1957–8

# Make a tessellating art gallery

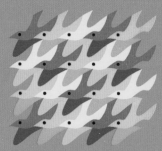

These three-pointed shapes will look good tessellating in contrasting colors!

Windmills also lock together easily!

These tessellating birds are all flying in the same direction.

Arrows will tessellate when they are placed pointing in opposite ways.

# MAGICAL MOSAICS
## make art from tiny tiles

Mosaics are pictures created from tiny pieces of glass, pottery, or stone. They have been made since ancient times.

Floors, walls, and sculptures can all be made of mosaic.

Some mosaics have survived for more than 3,000 years, buried under layers of earth.

## Make a mosaic

1 Find glue, scissors, and sheets of colored paper. Or use the strips on the next page.

2 Cut each sheet into hundreds of random tiny pieces—the shapes can vary.

3 Sketch a picture on a piece of white paper.

4 Color the picture using your little mosaic tiles.

### LOOK IT UP!

The Alexander Mosaic from Pompeii, c. 100 BCE

Antoni Gaudí, Park Güell, Barcelona 1900–14

Cut out these colored strips to make your mosaic tiles.

Pop out the frame to put around your artwork.

# USE PERSPECTIVE
## to make your pictures look 3D

When we look at a scene, things at the front appear larger, while objects in the distance look smaller. Artists use lines and grids to create this illusion.

The vanishing point is the place where things seem to disappear into the distance.

The horizon line cuts across the picture.

Objects at the front of the picture are larger, so appear closer. Things at the back are smaller, so look further away.

**LOOK IT UP!**

Paolo Uccello,
*The Hunt in the Forest*,
1470

Raphael,
*School of Athens*,
1505

## Draw a street using a vanishing point

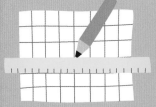 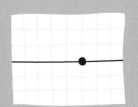 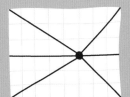 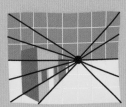

**1** Find some graph paper. Use a ruler to draw a horizon line.

**2** Draw a dot, or vanishing point, along the line. It doesn't have to be in the center!

**3** Draw lines from the dot to the corners and outer edges of the paper.

**4** Use these lines as a guide for placing buildings, windows, and people. Does your picture look 3D?

This scene is half drawn. Add some more trees,
a rabbit in the foreground, and more of the fence.

There are two vanishing points in this picture.
Can you spot them?

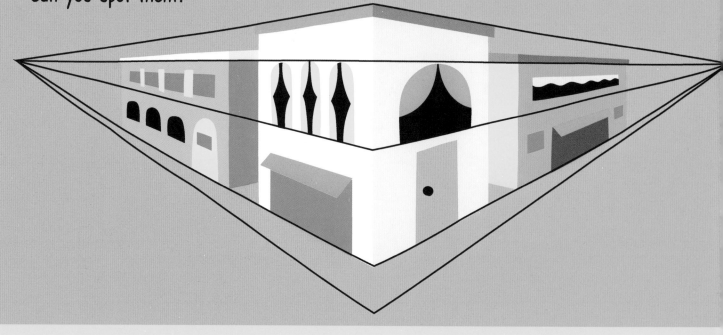

Can you label the horizon line and the vanishing point on this picture?

# MAKE ARTY MASKS
## to dress up and disguise!

Since ancient times artists have made masks that transform the wearer's appearance.

Masks feature in paintings, sculptures, and performances.

Masks are great for disguise. It's easy for someone wearing a mask to pretend to be someone—or something—else.

## Make an art mask

1 Cut out the masks on the next page. Press out the holes.

2 Thread some elastic through one hole and fix it with a knot.

3 Ask someone to help you to work out the length and tie the other end.

4 Decorate your mask. You can add fabric, wool, or sequins.

### LOOK IT UP!

Ad Minoliti,
*Biosfera Peluche/
Biosphere Plush*, 2021

Hew Locke,
*The Procession*, 2022

Cut out and decorate
these masks.

# LEARN POP ART SKILLS
## to create a bold picture

The *pop* in pop art stands for *popular*. In the 1960s, pop artists took images from the world around them—like photographs, magazines, or advertisements—and put them in their pictures.

This is a portrait of artist Go Suga—in many colors.

The same image, repeated, makes a striking picture.

## Make a pop art picture

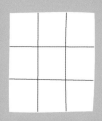

1 Divide a piece of paper into nine equal parts.

2 Find a photo of your face that is small enough to fit into one of the parts.

3 With tracing paper, trace the picture with a soft, slightly blunt pencil. Use as few lines as possible.

4 Turn the tracing paper over and trace the lines again.

5 Turn back to the original side. Position it in the right place on your picture.

Complete this
pop art picture by
finding images and
sticking them in all
the blank squares,
including this one.

a cartoon
character

a picture of a
famous person

a heart

some text from
an advertisement

a flag

a picture from
a magazine

a logo

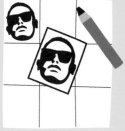

6 Trace over the lines a
third time. This time, your
picture will be transferred
onto the page!

7 Repeat, tracing your
photo into each square.

8 Go over the lines in
pen. Color in, using
zingy colors!

LOOK IT UP!
Pauline Boty,
*It's a Man's World I, 1964*
Andy Warhol,
*Marilyn Monroe, 1967*
Peter Blake,
*100 Sources of Pop Art,*
*2014*

# DRIP, SPLASH, AND SWIRL
## to make an abstract painting

When art is abstract, it doesn't look like something you immediately recognize. Some abstract artists use accidents and chance to make their paintings.

There's no design or drawing done beforehand.

The paint falls in random ways. Draw shapes quickly and go with the flow!

The paint is dripped, splashed, and splattered.

## Make a drip painting

1 Set up your paper where you can make a mess. If possible, go outside.

2 Choose paint that's runny enough to drip, but thick enough to make a mark.

3 Dip your brush in the paint and splash randomly. You can use both ends of the brush!

4 Draw lines, shapes, and circles in the air, and let the paint fall.

# Fold the fan and roll the tube. Fill them with paint and create!

Fan

Tube roll

## LOOK IT UP!

Jackson Pollock,
*Convergence*, 1952

Lee Krasner,
*Night Creatures*, 1965

## Make art tools

1. Cut out the fan template and fold it back and forth.

2. Squeeze one end to make the fan shape. Squeeze some paint into each groove.

3. Wave the fan to splatter the paint across a piece of paper!

4. Cut out the tube template, roll around a thick pencil, and tape into shape.

5. Pour paint down the tube and swirl it across the page.

# WOW, POP, ZING!
## explore complementary colors

17
Turn over
to make a
color wheel.

Colors look dramatically different when they are put next to contrasting tones. Exploring complementary colors will make your pictures bright and zingy.

Yellow pops out against purple.

Red looks bold next to green.

Orange appears bright against blue.

## Create pictures using different color combinations

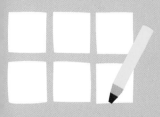

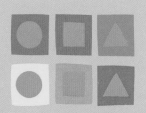

1 Draw six boxes on white paper. Try to make them all around the same size.

2 Inside, draw six simple designs and color them all the same shade.

3 Color the backrounds using the six shades from your color wheel on the next page.

4 Repeat, with new color combinations. How do the new colors affect your shapes?

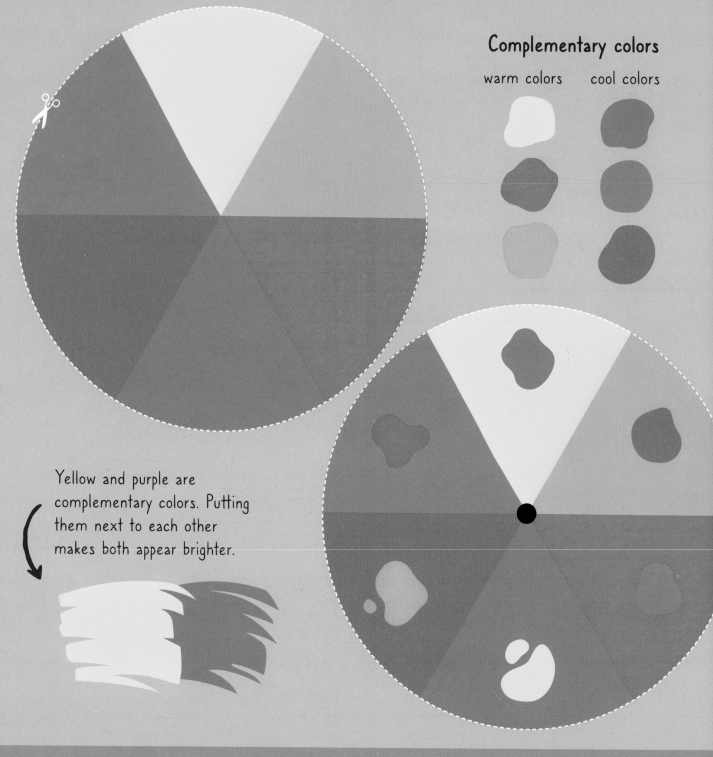

## Complementary colors

warm colors    cool colors

Yellow and purple are complementary colors. Putting them next to each other makes both appear brighter.

## Make a color wheel

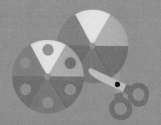

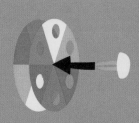

1. Cut out the two color wheels above. Press out the windows on the wheel that is perforated.

2. Put the wheel with the windows on top, and join the two wheels with a paper fastener.

3. Turn the wheel to work out which colors are complementary—you'll find them opposite each other.

### LOOK IT UP!

Vincent Van Gogh,
*Café Terrace on the Place du Forum, Arles at Night,* 1888

Georgia O'Keeffe,
*Anything,* 1916

# TURN IT INTO ART
## by creating "ready-made" artwork

Have an idea! Art doesn't have to be something you've drawn, painted, or sculpted. Sometimes it's the thought that counts.

Artists create "ready-made" sculptures by presenting real-life objects in a new way.

**The Acrobat**
Soft toy

Descriptions next to the artworks tell viewers what materials they are made from.

Choose your title carefully! It can be strange and intriguing or help explain the work.

**Mother and Child**
Two spoons

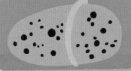

**Tied Down**
Balloon, rock, string

## Create a "ready-made" artwork

She Couldn't Stop Thinking About Football

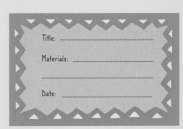

Title: ...............
Materials: ...............
...............
Date: ...............

1 Take time to choose some objects from around your home.

2 Decide how you'd like to display them. You can combine objects or present something on its own.

3 Experiment with placing your "ready-made" art on different surfaces—try a table, an easel, or a stand.

4 Use the labels on the next page.

Title: ..............................................

Materials: ..............................................

..............................................

Date: ..............................................

Title: ..............................................

Materials: ..............................................

..............................................

Date: ..............................................

Title: ..............................................

Materials: ..............................................

..............................................

Date: ..............................................

Title: ..............................................

Materials: ..............................................

..............................................

Date: ..............................................

Title: ..............................................

Materials: ..............................................

..............................................

Date: ..............................................

Title: ..............................................

Materials: ..............................................

..............................................

Date: ..............................................

Find these objects around the house and turn them into artworks.
You can combine them into one piece or make four separate works.

An object from
the kitchen.

Something with
a soft texture.

A round or
oval object.

Something square.

## LOOK IT UP!

Marcel Duchamp,
*Bicycle Wheel*, 1913

Jimmie Durham,
*Musk Ox*, 2017

# MAKE FLOATING ART
## by creating a kinetic sculpture

19
Turn over to make a floating, fluttering artwork.

Art that's kinetic is made of parts that move. String, wire, and folded shapes all create a hanging sculpture.

A wire structure holds everything in place.

Simple geometric shapes can be mixed with 3D cubes and prisms.

## Create a kinetic sculpture

1 You will need craft pipe cleaners, cotton or wool thread, scissors, and the templates on the next page.

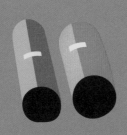

2 Turn over to cut out the flat shapes. Roll some of them into tubes.

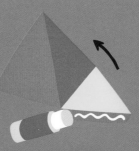

3 Cut out the pyramid template. Fold and glue into a 3D pyramid shape.

4 Make a frame out of pipe cleaners. Bend and twist the pipe cleaners to join them together.

# Cut out these shapes and make your own kinetic sculpture.

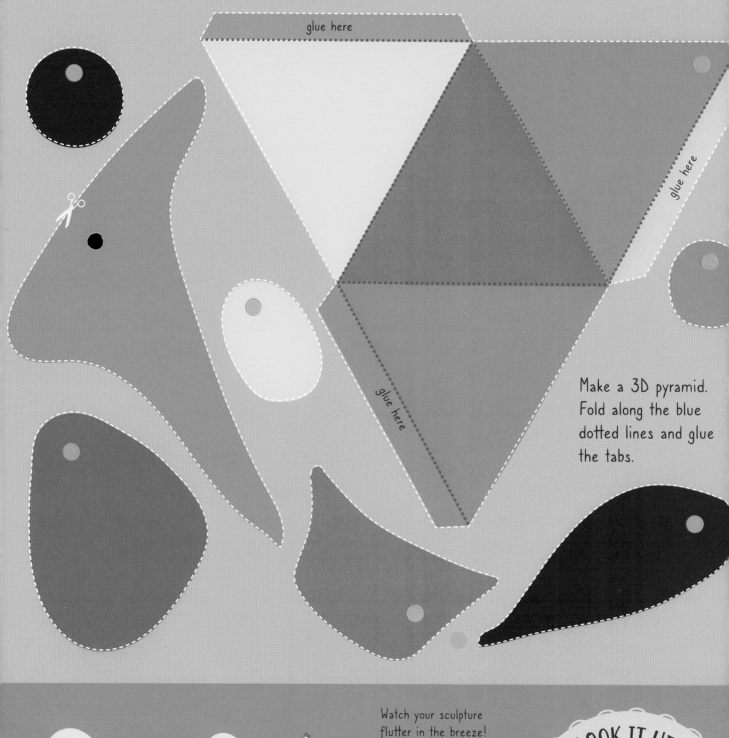

glue here

glue here

glue here

Make a 3D pyramid. Fold along the blue dotted lines and glue the tabs.

Watch your sculpture flutter in the breeze!

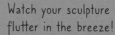

5 Thread the cotton or wool through the holes in your shapes and secure them with a knot.

6 Tie the other end of the thread to the pipe cleaner frame.

## LOOK IT UP!

Alexander Calder, *Peacock*, 1941

Beatriz Milhazes, *Marola*, 2010–15

# ALL IN A SPIN
## create eye-catching, revolving pictures
•

The designs on these discs make an even more dazzling display when they move and spin!

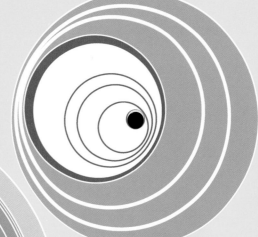

When shapes move fast, they blur and spin.

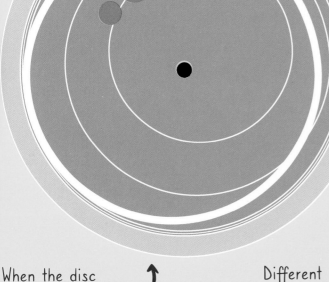

When the disc spins, colors mix and change.

Different patterns create new surprises.

## Make your own spinning art

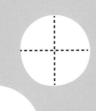

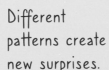

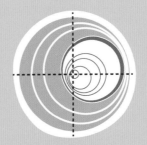

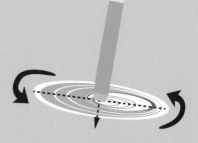

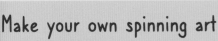

**1** Take a piece of paper and draw around a mug or cup to create a perfect circle. Cut out.

**2** Fold the circle in half and in half again. Unfold and mark the center point where the folds cross.

**3** Draw patterns on your paper circle and glue it onto some thin card.

**4** Pierce the center with a sharp pencil—and spin!

# Make your own spinning art!

Press out the pink dots, push a pencil through the middle, and spin!

When the discs spin, you'll discover new patterns.

## Try other inventive ways to spin your discs

If you can find one, try a record player!

Rub your hands together to move the pencil back and forth.

## LOOK IT UP!

Marcel Duchamp, *Rotoreliefs*, 1935

Martha Boto, *Eclipse Chromatique*, 1973

# CREATE CHARACTERS
## that move

Sequences of images that flash quickly in front of our eyes create the effect of objects or characters in motion.

Just a slight change each time makes the image appear to move.

## Make your own flip book

1 Grab a blank notebook.

2 Draw a picture on the bottom of every page.

3 Make very slight changes each time.

4 Flick through, and watch your character move!

**LOOK IT UP!**

Eadweard Muybridge, *Animal Locomotion*, 1887

Étienne-Jules Marey, *Bird in Flight*, 1886

Can you make a flip book of surfers?
Use the numbers to make sure that
the pictures are in the right order
and hold the left edge firmly.

Cut along the lines

1

2

3

4

5

6

7

8

9

# FOLD A SCULPTURE
## and make a paper work of art

Sculptures are 3D works of art.
They can be displayed in a gallery
or out in the open air.

You can walk around
a sculpture and
view it from many
different angles.

## Fold a creature sculpture

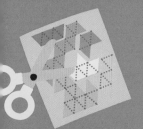

1 Cut out the creature
nets on the next page.

2 Fold along the blue
dotted lines.

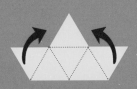

3 Can you make this
3D creature?

4 Try making this 3D
creature. Did you fold
inwards or outwards?

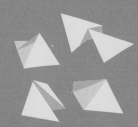

5 What other 3D
creatures can you make
with the templates?

# Use these nets to fold and create your own 3D creatures.

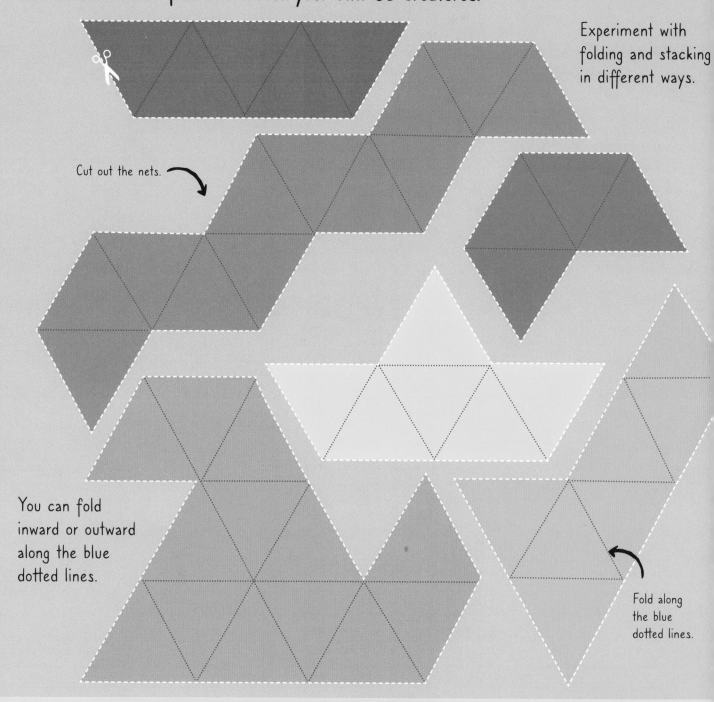

Experiment with folding and stacking in different ways.

Cut out the nets.

You can fold inward or outward along the blue dotted lines.

Fold along the blue dotted lines.

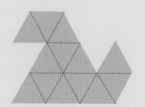  

**6** Which creature shapes can you make from the different nets?

**7** Experiment with folding in different ways before you settle on your creature shape.

**8** You can glue the 3D shapes together—and make even bigger creatures!

## LOOK IT UP!

Lygia Clark,
*Bichos,* 1960s

Isa Genzken,
*Elephant,* 2006

# USE A GRID
## to create a big picture

Artists use grids to copy and enlarge pictures.

This sketch is small enough to hold in the hand.

## Enlarge a picture using a grid

  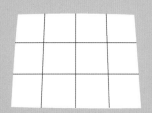 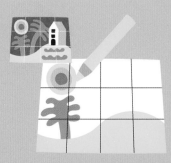

1 Find a picture you'd like to copy. It could be your own artwork or a picture from a magazine.

2 Using a ruler, draw a square grid over the top.

3 On a larger piece of paper, draw the grid again. This time, make the squares bigger.

4 Copy your picture, square by square. (Turn the page to find more pictures to copy!)

# Enlarge these gridded pictures.

Our illustrator, Go Suga, has started one for you already.

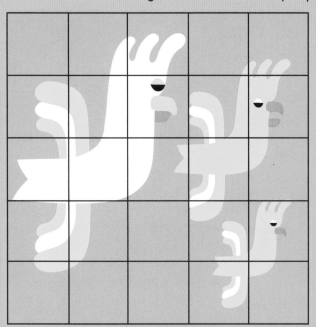

Finish enlarging the picture in the grid below by adding two more parrots.

# WORK TOGETHER
## to make art

**24**
Play a surrealist game with your friends.

Many artists enjoy making art as a group. It's a great way of dreaming up strange and wonderful pictures.

Accidents can add to the art.

Many artists can take part in making one picture.

Around 100 years ago, artists known as the surrealists enjoyed playing games to inspire their work.

Yves Tanguy

Wifredo Lam

André Breton

Jacqueline Lamba

## LOOK IT UP!

André Breton, Jacqueline Lamba, and Yves Tanguy, *Cadavre Exquis*, 1938

André Breton, Jacques Hérold, and Wifredo Lam, *Cadavre Exquis*, 1940

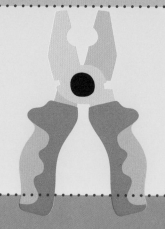

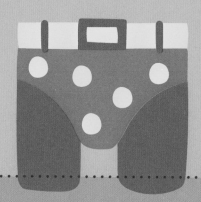

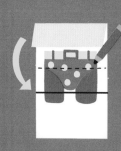

## Play a surrealist art game

1. Give your friends a piece of paper, folded into four equal parts.

2. In the top section, everyone draws a "head", folds the top in half to hide it and passes it on.

3. Draw a body in the next section, fold in half and pass on.

4. Next, draw legs, fold, and pass on. Draw the feet in the final section.

5. Fold the final section. Pass on and each unfold your papers to discover your surrealist creature.

# WEAVE A PICTURE
## with wool and thread

Many artists use the age-old technique of weaving to create works of art. They create colorful patterned cloth using a loom to thread and knot lengths of yarn.

The vertical yarn is called the warp. It is threaded in a fixed position.

The horizontal yarn is known as the weft.

The weaver threads the weft through the warp.

## Weave a picture

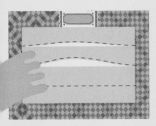

1 Cut out the loom on the next page. Press the perforated lines to make the slits.

2 Cut out the strips of paper.

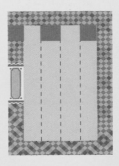

3 Weave a paper strip in and out of the loom, and push it to the top.

4 Weave the remaining strips. Make sure you alternate the start points as you go down to form the weave.

Gently push the perforated lines to make the splits in your weaving loom.

Cut out these strips to use with the loom.

**LOOK IT UP!**

Anni Albers, *Intersecting*, 1962

Otobong Nkanga, *Unearthed—Sunlight*, 2021

# CREATE A PICTURE
## without looking

It's fun to sketch quickly without thinking too hard! Drawings that focus on shapes, not details, are called contour drawings.

The artist looks straight ahead at their subject at all times.

Artists "feel" the drawing, using fast, continuous lines.

The pencil stays on the paper at all times.

## Make a contour drawing

1 Grab a pencil and paper and choose something to draw.

2 Focus straight ahead—don't look at the paper! Keep your pencil on the paper at all times.

3 Only look at the picture when you've completely finished!

### LOOK IT UP!

André Masson,
*Automatic Drawing*, 1924

Alice Neel,
*Hartley and Lushka*, 1970

Cut out these pictures. Can you copy them without looking down at the paper?

# SWIFTLY STENCIL
## to make bold works of art

Many artists use stencils to transfer their designs quickly onto the surface of the picture they are making—from paintings on canvas to murals on walls!

The same shapes can be colored differently each time.

They appear on their sides and even upside down.

## Make your own stencil art

1 Turn over to find your stencil kit. Cut along the lines and press out the shapes.

2 Choose a stencil and put it on a white piece of paper. Use sticky tack to keep it steady.

3 Paint over the stencil. Carefully remove the stencil to see the shape.

4 Add more shapes with other stencils to make a picture.

## LOOK IT UP!

Banksy,
*Girl with Balloon*, 2002

Sten Lex
410 Chamberlain St,
Atlanta, USA, 2012

Cut along the dotted lines and press out the shapes to make your Go Suga stencil kit.

# MIX IT UP
## to make a collage

A collage is an artwork made from lots of different cut-up images.

Images can be combined in unusual ways to make a totally new picture.

It's fun to cut out a variety of pictures from different places.

## How to make a collage

1 Collect some old newspapers, magazines, or photographs. Use the pictures on the next page, too!

2 Cut out random images and shapes. Don't think too hard about the images you're selecting.

3 Tearing and folding can create interesting textures—but neatly cut lines are good, too.

4 Stick them together to make a collage.

26

**5** Focus on surprising combinations.

**6** You can combine with paint and drawing.

Face Mask

**7** Give your picture a title!

## LOOK IT UP!

Hannah Höch, *Watched*, 1925

John Stezaker, *Mask XIV*, 2006

Deborah Roberts, *The Unseen*, 2020

# USE SYMMETRY
## to make a bold composition

A symmetrical picture is one that has identical matching parts. They face each other, as if in a mirror.

Everything on one side of the picture is perfectly mirrored on the other.

## Make a symmetrical picture

1 Fold a piece of paper in half and then unfold.

2 With thick paint, quickly sketch patterns and shapes on one side.

3 While it's still wet, fold the paper again to make an impression on the other side of the picture.

4 Open carefully to reveal your symmetrical picture!

### LOOK IT UP!

Andy Warhol, *Rorschach*, 1984

Sarah Morris, *Reflecting Pool (Capital)*, 2001

Complete these symmetrical pictures by drawing the mirror image.

# PUT ON AN EXHIBITION
## to display your pictures

Art is best when shared with friends. Exhibitions are public displays of works of art.

Moonlight

From Red to Yellow

Self-Portrait

Vase No. 1

Portrait of a Boy

Captions describing the art on the walls are useful for visitors to the exhibition.

She Couldn't Stop Thinking About Football

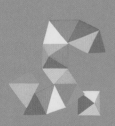
Tied Down

Snakes Alive!

## Design an exhibition poster

**THE COLOR SHOW**

Venue: School
Date: 2 May
Time: 3.00pm

**1** Think of a title for your exhibition, and choose your favorite work!

**2** Draw them on the poster—use bold lettering!

**3** On the poster, remember to include the venue, date, and time.

**4** Display the poster for all to see! Use the invitations on the next page to give to your friends.

COME TO MY ............................ EXHIBITION

Artist ...................................................................

Venue ...................................................................

Date and time ...................................................................

COME TO MY ............................ EXHIBITION

Artist ...................................................................

Venue ...................................................................

Date and time ...................................................................

COME TO MY ............................ EXHIBITION

Artist ...................................................................

Venue ...................................................................

Date and time ...................................................................